Fast Facts About

Fast Facts About
LABRADORS

by Marcie Aboff

raintree
a Capstone company — publishers for children

Raintree is an imprint of Capstone Global Library Limited, a company incorporated in England and Wales having its registered office at 264 Banbury Road, Oxford, OX2 7DY – Registered company number: 6695582
www.raintree.co.uk
myorders@raintree.co.uk

Text © Capstone Global Library Limited 2021
The moral rights of the proprietor have been asserted.
All rights reserved. No part of this publication may be reproduced in any form or by any means (including photocopying or storing it in any medium by electronic means and whether or not transiently or incidentally to some other use of this publication) without the written permission of the copyright owner, except in accordance with the provisions of the Copyright, Designs and Patents Act 1988 or under the terms of a licence issued by the Copyright Licensing Agency, 5th Floor, Shackleton House, 4 Battle Bridge Lane, London SE1 2HX (www.cla.co.uk). Applications for the copyright owner's written permission should be addressed to the publisher.

Edited by Megan Peterson
Designed by Sarah Bennett
Picture research by Kelly Garvin
Production by Tori Abraham
Originated by Capstone Global Library Ltd

978 1 3982 0290 0 (hardback)
978 1 3982 0289 4 (paperback)

British Library Cataloguing in Publication Data
A full catalogue record for this book is available from the British Library.

Acknowledgements
Capstone Press/Karon Dubke, 20; Getty Images/Smith Collection/Gado, 19; iStockphoto/AtomStudios, 15; Shutterstock: 279photo Studio, back cover, Annette Shaff, 11, BW Folsom, cover (left), el-ka, 18, FREEDOMPIC, 12, Gordon Mackinnon, 16, khrystyna boiko, 4, Kirk Geisler, 9, Natalia Fedosova, cover, NotarYES, 17, Radomir Rezny, 7, stocksre, 5, Susan Schmitz, 6, Vladimir Staykov, 13
Artistic elements: Shutterstock: Anbel, Vector Tradition

Every effort has been made to contact copyright holders of material reproduced in this book. Any omissions will be rectified in subsequent printings if notice is given to the publisher.

All the internet addresses (URLs) given in this book were valid at the time of going to press. However, due to the dynamic nature of the internet, some addresses may have changed, or sites may have changed or ceased to exist since publication. While the author and publisher regret any inconvenience this may cause readers, no responsibility for any such changes can be accepted by either the author or the publisher.

Printed and bound in India

Contents

The lovable Labrador 4

Labrador history 8

Labrador talents 10

Keeping Labradors healthy 14

Caring for Labradors 16

Fun facts about Labradors 18

    Make a dog toy 20

    Glossary 22

    Find out more 23

    Websites 23

    Index 24

Words in **bold** are in the glossary.

The lovable labrador

The Labrador retriever is a lovable dog. Labradors are happy to be part of a family. They are friendly to people and other dogs. Labradors are the second most popular dog **breed** in the UK.

Labradors make great pets. They are playful and clever. They like to run and swim. Labradors love chasing and catching balls. They bring balls back to you.

A Lab's fur can be yellow, black or brown. Labs have a **double coat**. The topcoat is rough. The bottom coat is soft and thick. Their fur keeps them warm in cold weather.

Labs are big dogs. They weigh 25 to 35 kilograms (55 to 80 pounds). They stand 56 to 60 centimetres (22 to 24 inches) tall. They are a similar size to golden retrievers.

Labrador history

The first Labs came from Canada. Labs **fetched** ducks for hunters. They helped bring in fishing nets. Years later, people in the UK raised Labs to do the same jobs. Now they are very popular as family pets.

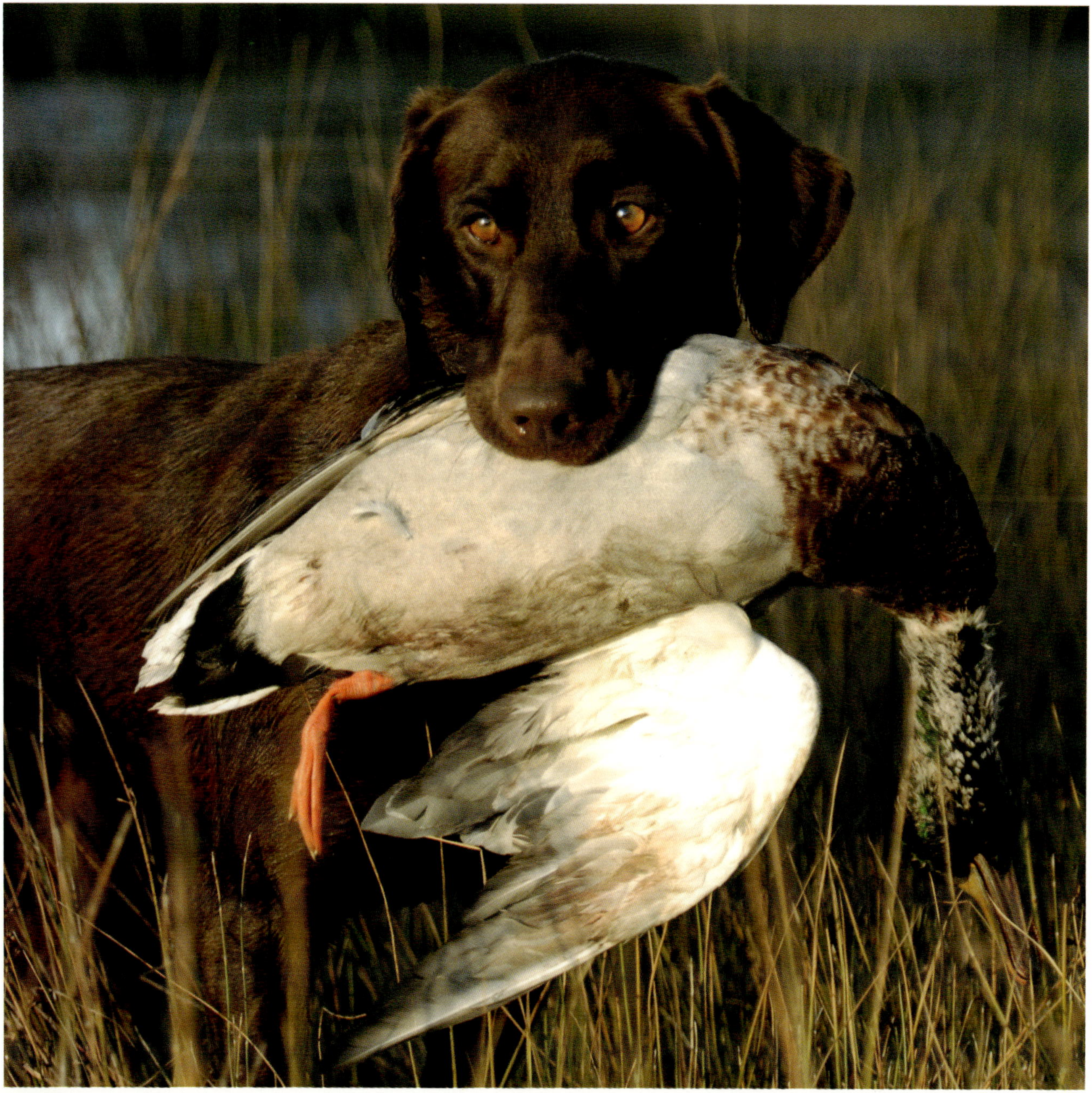

Labrador talents

Labs have many talents. They are great swimmers. They have webbing between their toes. This webbing helps them to swim. Labs have wide tails like an otter. The tail swishes back and forth. It helps them turn quickly when swimming.

webbing

11

Some Labs work as **service dogs**. They are trained to help their owners. Labs help people who are blind. They lead them around busy places. They help them to cross roads.

Labs also make good rescue dogs. Labs can find people who are lost. They save people who are hurt. Labs have a strong sense of smell. They follow a person's scent.

Keeping Labradors healthy

Labradors are a playful and healthy breed. They still need to visit the **vet** yearly. A vet takes care of animals. They help keep them healthy. The vet will check a Labrador's eyes, ears, lungs and heart. Labradors usually live for about 10 to 12 years.

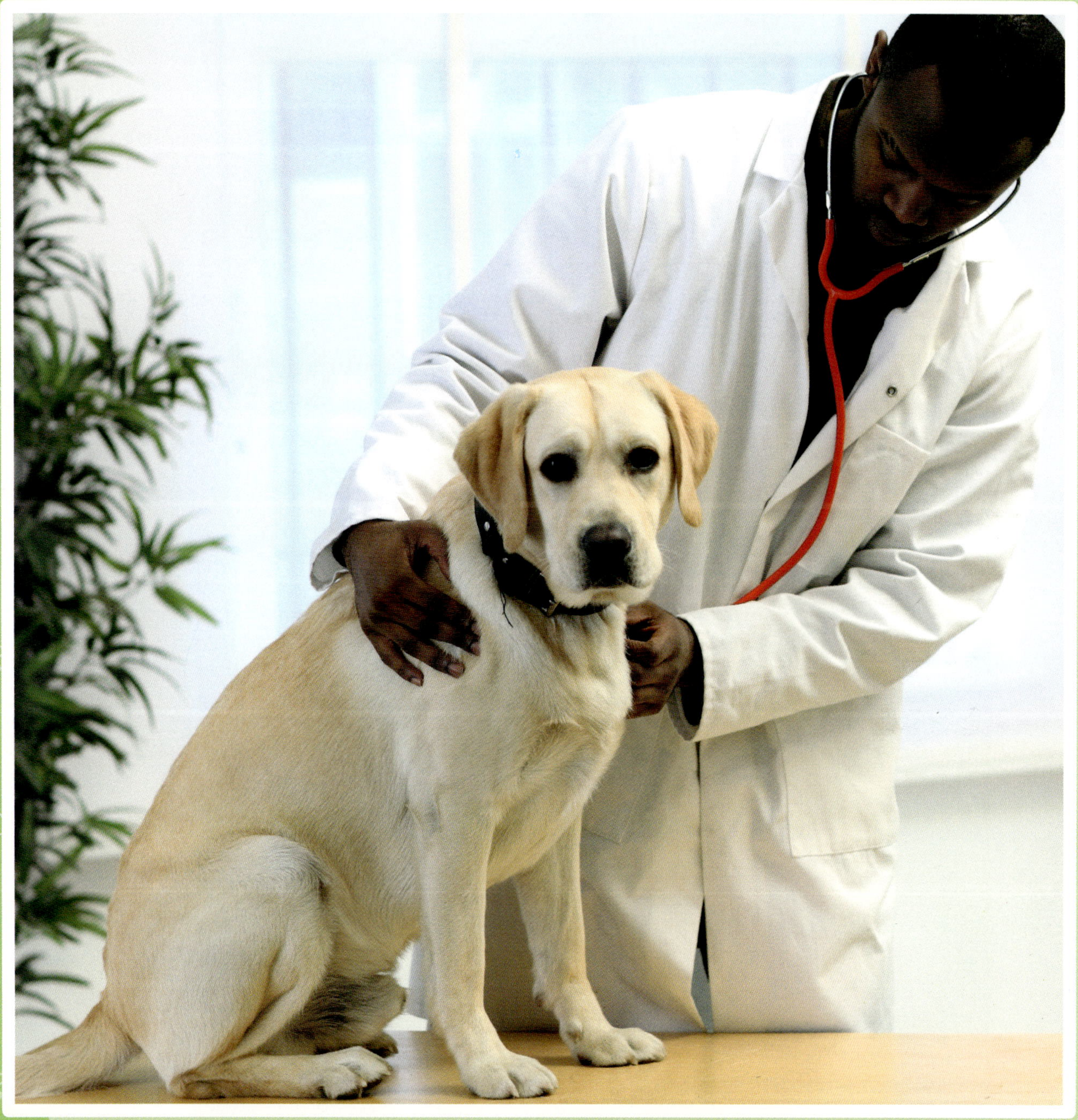

Caring for Labradors

Labs are the life of the party! They have a lot of **energy**. They need **exercise** every day. Puppies need to be trained. An untrained Labrador might chew up your shoes!

Labradors like to eat. Sometimes they eat too much! Be careful not to overfeed your Labrador. Brush your Lab every day. They shed a lot. Their teeth should also be brushed daily. Use a dog toothbrush and toothpaste.

Fun facts about Labradors

- One **litter** of Lab puppies can have all three fur colours.

- Labs are not good watch dogs. They are too friendly to strangers!

- Former US president Bill Clinton had a pet Lab called Buddy.

- Labradors are the most common breed trained as guide dogs.

Make a dog toy

What you need:

- scissors
- about half a metre of cloth
- an old ball, such as a tennis ball
- a piece of ribbon

What you do:

1. Cut the cloth into two equal strips. Lay the strips in an X on the floor.

2. Set the ball in the centre of the X. Fold the strips in half around the ball.

3. Tie the ribbon tightly around the cloth at the base of the ball.

4. Cut the tails of the cloth into many strips.

5. Plait the strips together. Tie knots at the end of the plaits with extra cloth.

Glossary

breed a certain kind of animal within an animal group

double coat a coat that is thick and soft close to the skin and covered with lighter, silky fur on the surface

energy the strength to do active things without getting tired

exercise a physical activity done in order to stay healthy and fit

fetch to go after something and bring it back

litter a group of animals born at the same time to the same mother

service dog a dog trained to help a person who is disabled

vet a doctor trained to take care of animals

Find out more

Amazing Dogs, Laura Buller (DK Children, 2016)

Spaniels, Retrievers and Other Gundogs (Dog Encyclopedias), Tammy Gagne (Raintree, 2018)

The Truth About Dogs (Pets Undercover), Mary Colson (Raintree, 2017)

Websites

DK Find Out: Domestic Dogs
www.dkfindout.com/uk/animals-and-nature/dogs/domestic-dogs/

Kiddle: Labrador Retrievers
kids.kiddle.co/Labrador_Retriever

The Kennel Club: Labrador Retriever
www.thekennelclub.org.uk/search/breeds-a-to-z/breeds/gundog/retriever-labrador/

Index

body parts 6, 10

care 14, 16–17

exercise 16

feeding 17
fur 6, 17, 18

history 8
hunting 8

rescue dogs 13
running 5

service dogs 12
size 7
swimming 5, 10, 18

training 16